CONTENTS

ACKNOWLEDGEMENTS 5

PREFACE 7

PART I - Method Explanation 14

CHAPTER I : PRACTICAL PHYSICAL EDUCATION 15

CHAPTER II : THE FOUNDATIONAL ELEMENTS OF ANY PHYSICAL EDUCATION METHOD 19

CHAPTER III : THE TRAINING METHOD 23

CHAPTER IV : MODEL SESSION 28

CHAPTER V : HOW TO DESIGN A PRACTICAL TRAINING SESSION 32

CHAPTER VI : HOW TO ESTABLISH A TRAINING PROGRAM 35

CHAPTER VII : RESULTS ANALYSIS 38

CHAPTER VIII SCORING & RECORD KEEPING 43

CHAPTER IX : HYGIENIC RECOMMENDATIONS 46

CHAPTER X : CONDUCTING GROUP INSTRUCTION 52

CHAPTER XI : FIELD ORGANIZATION FOR THE PRACTICE OF PHYSICAL EXERCISES 58

SPECIAL THANKS 68

ACKNOWLEDGEMENTS

The content of this book is easily a few hundred years old, as the translated work itself is based off already then known ways to train, which can date as far back as the Antiquity. Fitness began as military/martial training (for the goal of warfare). Roman legionnaires or the "Barbarian hordes" they would fight come to mind, while others can be found on "decorative documentation" (prior to the existence of manuscripts) on vases for instance. Below is an Etruscan vase depicting a trainer, recognizable by his forked staff, with annotations pertaining to the importance of a trainer in those times.

Athletic contests were central to the ancient life as part of religion and funerary rituals. Estruscans frequently decorated their tombs with brightly painted panels that often depicted athletic subjects. This image of a trainer to the right belonged to a much larger scene that was probably painted in such a tomb.

At the prompting of Dr Ed Thomas, I took it upon myself to translate the original works. French being my native tongue, it made sense to combine my culture with my profession, capturing language and training nuances at once. This is the first of three books, with each subsequent book more content rich than the first. Consider this first book the exposition to the method outlined by Hébert. Once again, while many of the exercises and training ways are not new, at the time, the structuring of the method through field-testing into a comprehensive, scalable and adaptable system is what gives this practical guide its value.

I found it particularly interesting that the methods outlined in the book (published in 1909) have run parallels in other countries, notably Germany and Sweden, as well as in the USA with the works of Stan LeProtti's program at the LaSierra High School, whose program was adopted throughout the United States after an appearance on the Tonight Show in 1962. I have myself received education throughout my professional career as a trainer in Russian methods with Pavel Tsatsouline. Many stem from military training, as it was a functional way to get individuals fit for combat.

The Natural Method, a Practical Guide to Physical Education has no other goal than to allow the individual to develop into a completely functional athlete. The incidental, well-defined and balanced muscular development, the associated sense of discipline and civic duty, instant readiness for action is the ultimate goal of the method. This is not a book outlining how to add inches to your pecs or biceps, or how to deadlift twice your bodyweight or cut 30lb of fat in 30 days, which are single-minded goals. There is no hype or marketing, just a simple, scalable and methodical way for a person of sane mind and body to achieve their athletic potential. Some might even call it "tactical".

With the advent of technological comforts, an increasingly sedentary lifestyle (already presented as an issue in the beginning of the 20th century) resulting in a regression of our physical fitness paired with the removal of humans from the food chain (a "massive upgrade" as comedian Louis C.K. likes to point out), the need for fitness on a daily basis is gone. However, it is vital to our health to seek that development. Hébert doesn't just focus on the physical development of the body from an aesthetic or functional standpoint, he also promotes the civil duty of the individual in order to be able to defend family, community and ultimately, country. This constitutes the *Noble Cause*, which this book is only a part of. With the assistance of my own peers and their parallel research, the goal is to share the knowledge and make it as widely available as possible.

My desire to undertake the massive task of translating Hébert's work is my personal duty and choice, with no goal for actual profit. The information belongs in the public domain and I encourage you to share this information with anyone interested. The low cost of the book has only the goal of making the information accessible in English, any revenue is purely a bonus. Why not make it completely free? Simply because without at least some assigned value, there is little incentive or commitment from the reader to complete the reading. It is out of respect for Georges Hébert, who truly pioneered physical education.

PREFACE

Hébert's "master" thought when writing the *Practical Guide to Physical Education* was to compose, or more precisely codify a method, a practical system with complete *physical perfection** as final educational goal, by the most effective, quickest and simplest means. (**Translator's note: the perfecting of the physical body through abilities and symmetrical, balanced muscular development. There is a subtle nuance in the French language where the word "improvement" and the root of the word "perfect" are degrees apart, as one is intended to lead to the other, improvement being the path to perfection)*

The method hereby presented is not a theoretical essay, meaning it was not composed at a desk. Quite the opposite, it was taught and practiced in the field; it is the outcome of a daily and personal practice over five years dedicated to the physical education of thousands of subjects of all ages, all builds, all occupations and origins, broken down into the following:

- 5000 subjects from 17 to 25 years of age (School of Marine Fusiliers of Lorient)
- 2000 subjects from 14 to 17 years of age (Brest maritime school)
- Several hundred children ages 7 to 14, active in sports.

This method has yielded sufficient evidence of its merits. Its excellent results, officially observed in the naval military schools, ended up being approved and adopted as a standard in the Navy.

Apparatus height: high elevation for high standards of performance.

It is however important to stress that the exercises that go along with the method are not new. Through the ages and countries where physical culture has been honored, the execution of the exercises has been nearly identical, give or take a few variations. For instance, trunk flexion and extension, running, jumping, swimming etc. share the same platform. Nearly all types of exercises have been tried and applied.

Moreover, progress in physical education doesn't consist of inventing movements of a specific nature, rather to distinguish, by experimentation, meaning a precise knowledge of their effects, which of them are the best exercises; to appropriately combine and blend them in order to reach, as quickly as possible, physical perfection; in the end, it mainly consists of a *better way to train.*

The Method comprises:

1) A *Basics* portion, made up of eight groupings of exercises, called *functional basics*, which consist of: marching, running, jumping, swimming, climbing, lifting, throwing, defense by natural means.

2) A *Preparatory* portion, where exercises with specifically targeted benefits for the various body parts can be found, consisting of: all the simple and combined movements of the arms, legs and trunk, facilitated by the normal function of the joints, suspension work, supported work, balance work, hopping/jumping and breathing.

3) A *Complementary* portion: games, sports of all kinds and common manual labor.

The eight groups of *basic functional* exercises that make up the main portion of the physical education suffice in allowing the individual to always be able to cope in difficult circumstances, as well as achieve the highest degree of physical aptitude However, not all share the same importance. It is evident that exercises that are geared towards the development of strength and the increase of cardiopulmonary power output are the most practical. Running, which combines these elements is, as outlined in the system/method, the first of the *educational exercises.*

The exercises called *basic educational* promote the methodical development of all the body parts. In consideration of the final goal of physical education, it is important to not misunderstand their place, nor to exaggerate their value. They may very well deliver a vast portion of the benefits of the basic functional exercises, but are absolutely insufficient by themselves to achieve complete physical perfection.

Analytically developing muscles and organs will not produce the *coordination* necessary in practical applications and uses.

Games, sports and manual labor provide completion/finality to all methodical training and promote the abilities required in all aspects of physical fitness.

The working method is both simple and practical. It is suitable for all: children as well as adults, individual as well as group instruction. It can be easily applied in any venue: at school, corporate environments, the Military. It requires no special equipment. It relies more on the "know how", the rational use of the available means rather than on gear, location or terrain.

It is important to note that *resistance to cold and poor weather* is part of the physical education and introduced during training. This portion happens naturally, by working out shirtless as often as possible* and by taking *air baths* throughout the seasons (*Translator's note: ladies will obviously used their discretion on this one…). Air baths are a powerful means of building resilience, vitality and a healthy constitution. Having observed its benefits from ongoing use, it cannot be recommended enough.

In summary, the method is essentially practical, building strong individuals capable of performing all kinds of functional exercises and possessing a minimum aptitude requirement when it comes to age and constitution. This minimum requirement is clearly defined.

One of the most unique and important aspects of the method lies in determining the *physical aptitude* and the *observation of results.* It is indeed necessary to be able to know at any given moment what an individual is capable of in actuality and to have a clear notion of the individual's physical power, or if desired, the person's absolute strength.

A *scorecard* was created to record the results of twelve classical tests, rated according a specific scale called the *aptitude scale*. The twelve tests are combined in such a way that their sum helps determine fairly precisely, through a numerical grading, the general physical value or the degree of physical aptitude of any individual.

If you consider that the principal elements of physical power, or absolute strength, are: muscular strength per se, agility as well as mental and neural energy, it becomes evident that to determine or evaluate this with numbers only could be a difficult problem to solve.

There is no claim to provide a solution here, or to have found a definitive formula to rigorously evaluate the power of the human machine. However, through the close study of the tests on the scorecard, which themselves have a specific choice of drills, we can obtain a fairly close measure of one's physical aptitude.

Only a longer experimentation will allow the completion or modification of this scorecard by adding, if necessary, a *coefficient* (or weight) to each test.

The scorecard shows the following in the aptitude tests:

1) Sustained strength is evaluated through 5 tests: the 100-meter sprint (speed), the 500-meter run (distance & speed), the 1500-meter run (distance), 100-meter swim, underwater breath hold (pulmonary strength).

2) In the event that several individuals obtain a similar score, from a general physical fitness valuation, defensive tactics such as boxing and wrestling are introduced in order to differentiate them. In other words, with equal general physical fitness, the strongest individual is the one winning the defensive tactics testing.

3) This process immediately creates *emulation* by clearly indicating the goal to reach; by giving everyone their measure of fitness; also by providing the weak ones their level of poor performance, which in turn is intended to stimulate their self-confidence and motivation.

This method is designed in such form that with only the notions in this book, without possessing any superior physical aptitude, any superior knowledge, it is quite possible to teach and conduct all the physical exercises in a very rational and methodical fashion.

The role of the educator is certainly a delicate one: it can only be fulfilled with rigorous perfection by individuals prepared solely for this function with a profound knowledge of anatomy, physiology, hygiene and the science of biomechanics. Furthermore, they need to be seasoned, well-rounded practitioners themselves. This category of *specialists* is still extremely rare.

Such specialists are of course necessary in order to provide a clear educational direction, in order to progress and help or train coaches and instructors. But, under the pretext that such individuals are lacking, one mustn't be under the impression that physical education is riddled with insurmountable challenges and that it is a domain strictly reserved to specialists. The idea, quite contrary, is that anyone already in a like position: parents, schoolteachers, professors, officers, company directors, etc., can quite perfectly, with the aide of this book, conduct the instruction of the physical exercises.

They simply need to deeply immerse themselves in the methodology, followed by the firm *will* power to train themselves. They will quickly realize that one doesn't need to be exceptional in order to walk, run, jump, swim, etc., or to correctly perform the majority of the exercises.

They must, in addition, themselves be of the conviction that it begins first with training and safety, then prevention and thus be capable of achieving excellent results. There is no instance of individuals who, with arduous training and perseverance for a necessary duration of time, didn't achieve significant improvements, if not to perfection, at least to an acceptable minimum.

Physical education begins during youth and continues through adulthood. Once perfection *(Translator's note: again, the notion of perfection lies in the ability to perform with correct form and technique)* is achieved, only maintenance is required in order to stay in shape and healthy with solid hygiene and a sufficient dose of training.

It is in everyone's best interest to start training as early as possible, because children who begin training early always become robust adults. Nevertheless, even at an advanced age, one can undergo physical "re-education" successfully, under the guidance and direction of a medical professional. Results will evidently not be as good, but they will be noticeable.

All forms of basic functional training can be practiced by children, as long as the training volume and duration is intelligently regulated, and that a slow progression is consciously observed not only in the performance, but more so during the skill development stage. Any exercise can be difficult if it is rendered so.

One mustn't be, as often observed, too apprehensive with the subject of functional exercise with youths.

As a matter of fact, children must be able to cope with difficult situations as soon as age permits. Just like an adult, they need to be able to escape danger, to help a friend in need, to defend themselves against a peer, etc. As is quite often the case, children instinctively seek exercises considered more "daring".

Despite the fact that this book was initially written for the male population, young girls and adult women can practice the majority of the exercises contained in it, especially the basic educational exercises.

Of course, the individuals participating in the described exercises need to be of sane mind and constitution, including hernias, heart disease etc.. With the latter, artistic and crafty side of instruction needs to be tapped into with common sense as to what needs to be done.

In conclusion, it is important to add that a thorough physical education doesn't consist only of teaching and training, but it also includes:

- Maintenance of proper hygiene and health.
- The teaching of physical duties, which one can call a "moral code of conduct".

This portion of the education, so important because it affects one's whole existence, ought to be delegated to medical professionals.

Complete physical education comprises the development of *moral and virile qualities* that turn boys into *men*. In order not to thicken this book, these qualities are only mentioned rather than examined in detail how to achieve them. But it is important to stress that moral education is inseparable from purely physical education. The school of physical fitness needs to also be the school of energy, will, courage, self-control and proactivity. The educator needs to lead by example, fighting laziness, softness, and inactivity and cultivate in everyone their love for training with a healthy desire for emulation.

Seeking strength, not just physical but mental, such is the duty of every human towards self, family, country and humanity as a whole. Only the strong remain useful in times of need, in dangerous situations, wars or any troublesome circumstances.

Under normal physical circumstances, there is no reason, no excuse to remain weak since methodical and steady work allows one to become strong. As indicated earlier, this is both a social as well as individual responsibility. To be able to help facilitate such achievement is the purpose of this book.

How the old gyms looked like: plenty of open space to hang from and move freely.

PART I - METHOD EXPLANATION

CHAPTER I : PRACTICAL PHYSICAL EDUCATION

Definition. Foundations. Purpose. Using the method for P.E. Natural education and natural method.

1. Activity is a law of Nature. Every living being, obeying an innate need for natural activity, reaches complete physical development by the mere usage of locomotion, as well as manual labor and defense mechanisms.

    Humans, in their most natural and primitive state, in the wild for instance, are compelled to lead an active life in order to sustain their needs, fulfilling complete physical development by only performing natural and functional exercises: walking, running, jumping, climbing, lifting, throwing, swimming, self-defense etc, as well as the partaking in mundane activities.

2. This incidental development is generally adapted to the needs and conditions of the environment in which the individual is required to inhabit.

    The value of this development varies depending on the original abilities of the individuals, their more or less active temperament, their strong (or not) constitution, the climate conditions of the location in which they dwell, the hardships met to sustain to their needs or maintain watch for safety.

3. In civilized countries, social obligations, conventions and judgment distance men from their natural outdoors environment and often prevent the practice of physical activity. Physical development falls behind, even can be stalled by said obligations or conventions.

    Those in modern society who are able to allocate a sufficient daily dose of training on par with what constitution can, without any particular method, reach full physical development by the simple practice of natural exercises and their variations and by performing basic functional drills or standard labor. This is a form of imitation of people living in a wild natural state, the difference being they do so by choice and leisure rather than out of necessity.

4. Such individuals are the exception. Generally, peer pressure and modern habits are such that, starting at a young age, physical activity is slowed down rather than encouraged. In addition, easy access to modern conveniences leads to physical laziness.

There are, however, many cases of individuals having reached near complete physical development without following any specific method. It is important to note that these individuals started with an excellent genetic make-up, and the means later used to achieve such results were the outcome of participation in games and sports that included running, walking, jumping, swimming and climbing, essential natural activities and their variations.

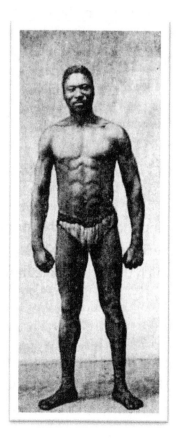 

Example of perfect and complete muscular development achieved without method but through natural means purely from performing functional and essential functions for his lifestyle. The individual in the picture is from the Saracolé people from Sénégal, living an outdoor existence, having to run, jump, swim, climb, lift, defend himself etc.

5. If, despite challenges, people living in civilized environments want to, while remaining loyal to their social conventions and obligations, reach complete physical development, they must comply with the following two principles:

    a. Dedicate a sufficient amount of time daily to cultivate the body.

    b. Optimally manage that time allocation in order to not do anything wasteful.

The ideal situation is to produce a dose of activity, in a given amount of time or the minimum amount of time, without negative effects on the body, more or less equivalent to that of a life being spent in the wild.

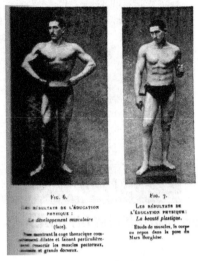

Hébert's Physique

6. The cultivation of the body, when done in a continuous and progressive manner, constitutes *physical education*. It can be done entirely with natural movement patterns, without order or methodology, the same as in people living outside of civilized areas. In that case, physical development is acquired randomly and its final measure and value is uncertain. For instance, many tribes living in the wild are under developed.

    The methodical or rational education is quite different. A method, as a matter of fact, a system, brings precision to training, avoids trials, removes what is unnecessary and controls the outcome. A system allows to move forward with certainty towards the proposed goal, which is the achievement of a balanced physique. Hence the benefits of a structured method, especially with time constraints, or among many, genetic afflictions.

7. The choice, order and regulation of exercises based on their known outcome on the body is what constitutes the teaching method.

    The non-civilized individuals begin by themselves through imitation, later garnering from their acquired experience; this action is entirely instinctual.

The method, on the other hand, helps the civilized individual from the get-go by indicating the best principles to follow. It allows to bypass many fruitless efforts and personal experience that can be wasteful or even dangerous. It allows to thus save time.

Moreover, one needs to realize that the effects of certain natural exercises or certain labors nearly impossible to execute can, in some cases, be obtained "artificially" by certain specific and determined movements. Such movements can never, however, truly replace their natural counterparts. They're mostly a *"patch"*.

Georges Hébert himself and his naturally developed back.

8. The systemized educational method's unique proposition is to allow the human machine to reach its maximum potential, or to put it simply, to forge strong people.

    From a practical standpoint, this translates into good health, energy, resistance to fatigue and illness and minimum necessary requirements to perform natural and functional exercises. These exercises form *eight distinct categories*: walking (marching), running, jumping, swimming, climbing, lifting, throwing and natural defenses (through boxing and wrestling).

    You only need a brief moment to reflect on this to understand that these eight categories are all useful, in various degrees, throughout our existence. Outside of them exists the practice of activities like fencing, horseback riding, rowing, which are of secondary use or limited to a certain population; or games, sports, acrobatic or fun activities, none of which are really needed for every single individual, regardless of social status or occupation.

    Henceforth, there is only one general system geared at the perfection of the human machine, and it is based on progressive training and the methodical practice of natural and functional drills. We can call it the *Natural Method*.

CHAPTER II : THE FOUNDATIONAL ELEMENTS OF ANY PHYSICAL EDUCATION METHOD

Educational portion and practical portion. Basic differences. Exercises respective to each portion.

Every physical training method contains:

1) An educational portion whose main role is to produce specific results on the body. It also tends to:

    a. Mechanically promote the enlargement of the thoracic cage and give it greater mobility.

    b. Increase lung capacity.

    c. Strengthen abdominal muscles.

    d. Normally develop the rest of the muscular system.

    e. Correct imbalances and bad habits, such as: rounded back, forward shoulders, exaggerated lumbar curve.

    f. Teach the optimal way of performing natural and functional exercises: marching/walking, running, swimming, climbing, lifting weights, throwing objects and defensive tactics.

2) A practical portion whose main role consists of:

    a. Developing skill to the highest level using strength and agility by applying the skills developed in the educational portion.

    b. Providing measureable results.

    c. Training the individual for readiness and coping abilities in real life.

Both portions of the method, despite their distinctive roles, are not definitively kept separate during practice; in other words, there is no set duration for teaching the educational portion alone. One links to the other, as a matter of fact; education and practical application can go hand in hand, especially with children. It all depends on the physical constitution, the aptitudes, the degree of training and the pace at which the individual progresses.

The educational portion can be extended for weak or uncoordinated individuals. For the more vigorous, athletic, daring and naturally resilient individuals, it is nearly without use.

Some may not even need the educational portion, be it for some specific drills only.

The educator is in charge of assessing the condition and ability of the individual, ensuring all elements are always in place before pushing instruction further along, to not go too fast and to not stay stagnant, or to not hesitate, if need be, to take a few steps back.

The educational portion contains the following exercises:

1) Basic arms, legs and trunk movements: elevation, flexion, extension and in general, all displacement of the various segments of the body permitted by the normal function of the joints and articulations.

    These movements can be performed either *free-hand (translator's note: in some systems, training without equipment is referred to as "naked")* or with portable equipment: dumbbells, wands, bars, mace, clubs, elastic tubing etc.

2) Simple hand suspension/hanging drills, including horizontal progressions, arms extended or flexed, legs raised or dropped. Suspension/hanging work can be done anywhere and on anything that the hands can hold on to.

3) Hand supported drills: on hands only or on hands and toes, arms straight or bent. Hand supported drills can be performed on anything (stool, bench, rock), or on the ground itself, with or without the help of the feet for added support. They can also be done on surfaces where the feet do not reach the ground (rings, high bar, etc...)

4) Single leg balance.

5) Single or double leg hops, in place or directional.

6) Breathing movements.

7) Natural movements or locomotion: walk/march, run, jump. Added: the mechanical performance of these natural patterns with breathing education during their execution.

8) Necessary useful exercises: swimming, climbing, weight lifting, object throwing, and defensive tactics. Optimal skill development for the performance of the above drills.

The practical application portion includes:

1) Natural movements: walk/march, run, jump, but performed in progressively more challenging circumstances; longer and faster walks or runs, on all sorts of terrain, flat or *off the beaten path*; jumping over or traversing real obstacles.

2) *Necessary functional exercises*: swimming, climbing, weight lifting, object throwing, defensive tactics, also performed with increasingly more difficult levels or nearing real life situations, such as:

    a. Swimming fully clothed.

    b. Crossing rivers.

    c. Climbing all sorts of obstacles.

    d. Boxing.

    e. Wrestling.

3) Rescue exercises:

    a. Water rescue.

    b. Resorting to any tools or available objects to climb over or clear obstacles.

    c. Transporting wounded individuals.

4) The practice of games and sports, starting with the most useful ones, after having completed exercises classified as necessary. Finally, mundane manual labor.

Non-necessary sports from a functional standpoint do not belong per se in the method of physical education. The only add to it very efficiently. It is evident that it would be hard pressed to introduce on a regular basis many different sports into the curriculum. Interest in additional sports remains the choice of the individual.

5) In summary, any physical education system or method contains the following exercises:

   a. *Basic educational exercises:* basic arm, leg, trunk movements, suspended or hanging work, supported work, balance work, hops[1] and breathing patterns.

   b. *Natural and necessary functional*, divided into 8 categories: marching/walking, running, swimming, climbing, lifting weights, throwing objects and defensive tactics.

   c. All sports and games, even for fun rather than useful function, as well as common manual labor.

---

[1] Translator's note: Hops or hopping is different from jumping drills. The language nuance lies in the effort produced for a broad or high jump, for instance, versus bouncing or hopping in place in a warm-up fashion, like jumping jacks or skipping rope.

CHAPTER III : THE TRAINING METHOD

General rules regarding the way to train. What constitutes a session or lesson of rational work. Choice, order and relative duration of the various exercises making up a lesson or session.

The combination of various drills, their classification, order of execution, relative duration and energy expenditure, all of it makes up the training "way".

In P.E., as in any other subject, results depend not just on the quantity of work delivered, but also in a large part on the *training method.*

It is not possible to define in an absolute fashion what this method ought to be; we can only do so with general principles and broad strokes.

Indeed, too many elements are in consideration in order to set everything in stone in advance. Hence: age, physical constitution, occupation (current or in preparation), time or geographical circumstances are among many factors that compel adjustments in the training method.

Some details are left to the instructor or coach. There is an art to training like there is to teaching and nothing can replace the value and experience of a Master instructor, as well as the arduous efforts and care brought on by the coach.

Physical training is usually regulated by sessions of a predetermined duration during which a designated amount of exercises are performed. This session is called a "lesson" when administered by a master or instructor.

A *rational* training session or lesson correctly conducted is not a juxtaposition or grouping of random exercises performed without rhyme or reason. There is a logical sequence of various exercises, arranged so as to address the various body parts according to their relative physiological importance in their later practical application.

The order of relative physiological importance of the various body parts is the following:

1) Lungs and heart.

2) Muscles responsible for the retraction of shoulders, rib elevation and straightening of any slouching and aligning of the spine (trapezius, dorsal and rhomboid muscles).

3) Abdominal muscles.

4) Muscles of the limbs.

The exercises with a functional application are those already mentioned in chapters I & II: walk, run, jump, swim, climb, lift, throw, defensive tactics.

The most important of them all is running, or racing, from both a practical standpoint (the ability to move quickly or for an extended period of time) and from a physiological standpoint (intense development of the cardiopulmonary system and putting nearly the entire muscular system in action). This is a fundamental exercise for P.E. through the Natural Method.

A session is considered completed when the execution of all the prescribed exercises deliver the following results: a hygienic effect, an aesthetic effect and a functional effect.

The hygienic effect is produced more specifically by the exercises that activate breathing and circulation and in general, by the efforts of the lesson's activities.

The aesthetic effect is produced by the exercises that develop the muscular system, which remedy poor shoulder position, expand the rib cage and bring the spinal curve back to its optimal alignment.

The functional aspect is the end result of the drills having a practical purpose: walk, run, jump, swim, climb, lift, throw, defensive tactics.

Generally speaking, a thorough session is the summary, or rather, the shortcut path of all disciplines contributing to the perfecting of the body.

In practice the ideal session is made up of all kinds of exercises:

1) Basic educational drills: basic arm, leg, trunk, suspension/hanging, support, balance, hops and breathing patterns.
2) Natural and functional: marching/walking, running, jumping, swimming, lifting, throwing, defensive tactics.

A *random* session needs to closely resemble an *ideal* session. If circumstances do not permit it, the minimum effective dose can be as follows:

1) Loosen up the trunk and limbs.
2) Develop or maintain the muscular system, particularly the back and abdominals.
3) Hanging/Suspension and support drills (planks, pushups).
4) Run/jog.
5) Jump.
6) Breathing work.

Even under the worst circumstances such as lack of time, space, equipment or other, a session or lesson ought to never be made up of exercises of a similar nature focused on one body part only. For instance, a session composed of only hanging drills would only work the upper body and trunk. Only swimming, which combines all the benefits listed so far, is the exception to the rule.

On another hand, long walks/marching, (which includes rucking, hiking) and sprints vs. distance runs, as well as certain games and sports can, in some cases, have a sufficiently thorough benefits value.

The order in which the exercises need to be performed is not random. It is based on energy expenditure or on the stress of the sequential work placed upon the body.

The session always begins with moderate exercises to get the engine started. Drills of increasing energetic expenditure then follow it; the session ends with a cool down and a reset of the body, restoring calm to the entire system. The ensuing fatigue needs to be the cumulative outcome of the work performed by all the body parts, not just the work from one body part or modality.

There is no absolute order, however. Its order depends on the decision to focus on particular exercises, outside of their intrinsic stress. Some drills, for instance, such as basic arm, trunk and leg movements output only a low level of energy expenditure, regardless of the energy solicited to perform them. Their ranking order is thus always at the beginning of the session, or during as *derivatives* or variety, to provide the body a sense of relative rest after more demanding drills.

Others, by contrast, such as hopping, sprints, jumps etc, put into action important parts of the human system. Their logical place s thus after less demanding exercises when the "organic machine" is sufficiently warmed up.

The general rule is essentially the following: increase effort gradually and do not finish abruptly.

The *total* duration of a session or lesson varies according to circumstances. In principle, an hour daily is sufficient to train and educate the body, if that time allotment is judiciously employed.

The relative duration allocated to the various exercises in regards to one another can vary greatly. It depends on:

1) The total duration of the session.

2) The stress and difficulty of the exercises or the fatigue they cause on the individuals.

3) The importance of the focus on certain exercises in order to produce specific desired results.

A session, or lesson, be it complete or not, really requires continuous and sustained training. Rest during the session needs to be reduced to a minimum.

In a perfectly conducted lesson, the sequence of drills is regulated in such a manner that rest is reduced to only seconds. Often indeed, no rest is necessary. The act of moving from one exercise to the next should provide the body the rest or relaxation necessary to continue training.

CHAPTER IV : MODEL SESSION

Exercise grouping by sections. Mutual goals and effects of each section. Logical order of performance of the various exercises.

In order to fulfill the requirements of a *rational* training session, outlined in the previous chapter, the exercises that constitute the method are grouped by section.

Exercises within a section have similar benefits or lead towards the same goal.

Each section or series is broken down into 7 drills. Their methodical order constitutes the *model* for a complete training lesson or session.

The chart in this chapter on the next page indicates the exercises of each section as well as their goal or mutual benefits.

The various directions of movement, a.k.a. *displacements,* during a training session are performed either by walking/marching or running.

The walking portion can be performed:

1) At the beginning of the session, as a warm-up or to go along with corrective exercises.

2) Within the training session, by starting or ending sprints or distance runs or any other strenuous exercise, as well as to be combined with the various arm movements (for coordination).

3) At the finish of the session, immediately after the breathing exercises or during their execution.

Walking/Marching therefore can be used in one of two ways:

1) As a functional exercise for locomotion or training.
2) As a derivative exercise to prepare the body for training, or to calm down the body after a strenuous effort.

In the latter case, walking on toes/ball of foot is suggested. *(Translator's note: there is no explanation as to the reason for this cue)*

Upon examination, the model session establishes that the plan is aligned with the given definition in the previous chapter of *"complete rational training session"*. Indeed:

1) The various exercise sections produce 3 essential benefits: hygienic, aesthetic and functional.
2) The order adopted for each section is optimal for performance. It is based on the concept of increasing then decreasing energy output.

See chart on next page

SECTION	EXERCISES	GOALS AND BENEFITS
1	1. Any kind of walking. 2. Corrective exercises. 3. Flexibility and mobility of the arms, leg and trunk.	Correcting mindset, warming up the body and general loosening up of the body (aesthetic benefits).
2	1. Basic arm and leg movements, simple or combined, free hand or with gear. 2. Lifting. 3. Throwing. 4. Combatives: boxing and wrestling.	General and symmetrical development of all the body parts. Joint flexibility (aesthetic benefits). Skill development and coordination in order to improve fighting, lifting and throwing abilities (functional benefits)
3	1. Suspension/Hanging. 2. Supported/Planks. 3. Climbing variations. 4. Balancing drills geared also at overcoming fear of heights/vertigo.	Specific development of the upper body, trunk and core musculature (aesthetic benefits). Sense of equilibrium, agility of all kinds for climbing or scaling (functional benefits).
4	1. Hopping. 2. Speed training. 3. Short distance runs.	Intense action on the major systems of the body: cardiovascular and respiratory (hygienic benefits). Improvement in normal and work pacing (functional benefits).
5	Trunk and core specific	Emphasis on back, thoracic and abdominal musculature development (aesthetic benefits).
6	1. Jumps of all kinds: with or without momentum, with hand support, on moving or fixed obstacles. 2. Velocity/speed and distance running (like in Section 4). 3. Swimming. 4. Games utilizing running, jumping, swimming, fighting actions etc...	Same benefits as in Section 4, but more intense. All the exercises in this section produce hygienic, aesthetic and functional benefits.
7	1. Breath work. 2. Marching/Walking.	Restore the cardiovascular and pulmonary systems. Breathing education.

Thus:

- Exercises in Section 1 simply serve to warm-up and loosen up the body.
- Exercises in Sections 4 and 6 on average require greater effort than those in Sections 1, 2 and 3.
- Section 5 is positioned on purpose between two sections of more strenuous nature (jumping, running etc.) because the exercises in this section require little effort but provide the body with the necessary relaxation characterized by a lowering of the heart rate.
- Finally, exercises in Section 7 are geared towards restoring the breath and lowering the heart rate before resting. They can be performed during the session when the taxing efforts of a particular exercise require restoration.

CHAPTER V : HOW TO DESIGN A PRACTICAL TRAINING SESSION

Category of exercises to perform. Complete vs. incomplete session.
Choice and order of exercises.

To design a thorough/complete training session according to the "model" means a choice needs to be made in picking one or several types of exercises in each section and performing them in the order of the sections.

Ideally, a complete lesson/session needs to have, as we have seen so far, the entire sequence of exercises according to the model. In practice, it consists of the successive execution of the 12 kinds of following drills:

SECTION 1: 1) Warm up by walking, adopting an upright posture and extending the limbs and trunk.

SECTION 2: 2) Train the muscles of the arms and legs also using all joints and articulations.

3) Lifts.

4) Throws.

5) Martial drills: boxing, wrestling, combatives, and defensive tactics.

SECTION 3: 6) Suspension and support exercises.

7) Climbing and scaling.

SECTION 4: 8) Hopping and running.

SECTION 5: 9) Back and abdominal muscles emphasis.

SECTION 6: 10) Jumps

11) Swimming (if possible logistically), running or games/sport.

SECTION 7: 12) Breathing exercises.

The order of execution of the various drills within each section is of secondary importance. Drills/exercises in sections 2 and 3 can even be alternated, since they possess similar benefits and are geared towards the same goal.

In general, to properly spread out energy expenditure while reducing rest to a minimum, two consecutive exercises of movements (*superset*) need to focus on different body parts.

Each category of exercises of the model itself contains *different kinds* of exercises or movements under the same *"denomination"*. I.e. performing suspended/hanging drills, jumping drills or trunk exercises means performing one or more various suspension drills, different kinds of jumps, several trunk exercises etc, each exercise or movement being performed for a given amount of repetitions.

If, for whatever reason, there isn't enough time, space or equipment or desired effect achievement, the session cannot be considered *complete*, i.e. it is not made up of the exercises from all the sections. One needs to always choose and arrange the exercises that form a complete session, as per the methodical order of the model.

For instance, a session comprised only of jumps or suspended exercises should be organized as the following:

1) Preliminary warming up and loosening/stretching exercises.
2) Suspension
3) Jumps
4) Breathing exercises.

Suspension drills are placed before jumping drills, because they are less rigorous than the latter and also because they belong in Section 3 of the model, whereas Jumps are classified under Section 6.

Preliminary/warm-up drills and breathing drills, because of their short required duration, can always be part of a session, even a short one.

The choice of exercises of a session also depends on:
1) The age of the participants.
2) Their general health and physical constitution.
3) Their level of fitness.
4) The level of difficulty achieved in preceding sessions.
5) The desired goals to achieve.
6) The weaknesses needing to be addressed or improved upon.
7) Weather conditions.
8) Ambient temperature.
9) Terrain or available equipment, etc.

CHAPTER VI : HOW TO ESTABLISH A TRAINING PROGRAM

Method of designing a progressing training plan. Variable adjustments according to results. General training and specialized training.

Consistent, methodical, progressive work constitutes *training*, meaning the path to the *end goal* of education: to provide the human machine its maximal and optimal capacity. Training must occur daily in order to be effective.

A progressive training plan consists of daily sessions of increasing difficulty. The difficulty is the outcome of the following gradation:

1) Choice of increasingly more difficult movements or exercises.
2) Total number of exercises in a session.
3) Relative rest.
4) Total session duration.

The same session can be made more difficult without changing any of its exercises:

1) By seeking a prolonged and more intense effort.
2) By reducing rest periods.
3) By increasing the cadence or speed of movements.
4) By adding repetitions.
5) Working with more vigor and expending more energy.

To establish sessions of increasing difficulty is the most delicate aspect of program design. The final results stem from the quality of such a program.

On one hand, to avoid overtraining, the body cannot be taxed too hard. To achieve that, the rules of *fatigue management* need to be followed.

On the other hand, there needs to be sufficient work in order to avoid stagnation or staleness. If the program is well designed, there should always be noticeable progress, or at least no regression after each training session.

A training program must be based on the immediate effects of certain exercises as well as the economy of muscular training. Any error or setback in the exercises can lead to a waste of time, loss of motivation or wasteful overtraining. If the progression is properly periodized, the individual naturally takes on more difficult exercises without undue effort. The inability to perform a given exercise always indicates that some preliminary exercises were either neglected or insufficiently repeated.

For instance, when it comes to scaling or climbing, to start with the more difficult obstacles is a gross technical error as well as a poor judgment call. One must begin climbing with a straight rope first in order to prepare. The straight rope engages all the "climbing" muscles. At first, the use of the legs can help these muscles gradually, even amongst the weaker individuals.

Likewise, the various jumping drills can only be performed when the legs have been sufficiently prepared, with safe landings by performing ordinary jumps.

Speed and power develop naturally by performing active relaxation and dynamic stretching.

(...)[2]

Of course, knowledge of proper care, nutrition is a requirement.

---

[2] (...) indicates a gap or missing information from the original document.

When an individual develops all of the aforementioned qualities to an exceptional degree, this person is considered an *athlete*.

We cannot possibly expect to develop all physical qualities to the fullest in all individuals in order to turn them into athletes. Two things work against that: firstly, the less than perfect physical constitution/genetic make-up of the majority of individuals. Secondly, our modern society's expectations, which only permit a limited amount of time to Physical Education.

CHAPTER VII : RESULTS ANALYSIS

Use of the analysis. Method of analyzing with periodical tests. Physical aptitude measure: sufficient, non-existent, internal, average, superior, exceptional. Minimum physical aptitude performance requirements for the complete athlete. Individual type card model.

The periodical observation and analysis of results is necessary to gather an accurate measure of the quality of work to date, as well as the effectiveness of the method.

Observation is conducted by comparative analysis. The difference in the quality of performance or accomplishment of exercises at two points in time provides a the quality of results achieved.

The general physical ability/aptitude can be measured by a series of exercises that are ranked and weighed according to a predetermined scale that would include, together or separately: muscular strength, conditioning and coordination. The necessary tests in order to determine this aptitude need to be comprised of the following, at the minimum:

1) Jumps (to measure agility, coordination and the extensibility of the lower limbs).
2) Running, for both distance and speed (conditioning)
3) Straight rope climb (muscular strength of the upper body, arms and core).

(...)

For an individual of at least 18 years of age and of normal constitution, performance should not rank below the following grading scale (which represents a score of 0):

High Jump without momentum	0.8m
High Jump with momentum	1m
Broad Jump without momentum	2m
Broad Jump with momentum	3m

Straight rope climb (without the use of the legs)	5m
100m dash	16 seconds
500m run	1min 40 sec
1500 meter run (1.5K)	6 minutes
Lifting of a 40kg/88lb weight or stone (deadlift)	1 time
Average of both hands of 7.2kg/16lb shot put/throw	5m
100m swim	3 minutes
Underwater breath hold	10 seconds

Walking can be added to these 12 tests in order to assess individuals with a natural exercise as such. However, this isn't a required test as it would be evident that anyone having the ability to run, jump and swim ought to be assumed as possessing adequate capability to walk, a form of exercise of a much less strenuous nature than the aforementioned three kinds. Marching/walking at this point becomes more a question of foot care and choice of shoes.[2]

For individuals ages 16-18, of normal physical constitution, scoring should not fall below a -1 in each event.

For individuals ages 14-16, scoring should not fall below a -2.

---

[2] The following standards can be considered as minimum requirement (on flat terrain without carrying any load) for walking:

Age 18	20km in 4 hours.
Ages 16-18	20km in 4 hours 30 minutes.
Ages 14-16	20km in 5 hours.
Ages 12-14	20klm in 6 hours.

Additionally, any adult of sane and average constitution ought to, in the same conditions, be able to cover 50km over the course of a 12-hour day.

Finally, for individuals ages 12-14, minimum scoring should be at -3, which corresponds to:

High Jump without momentum	0.5m
High Jump with momentum	0.7m
Broad Jump without momentum	1.7m
Broad Jump with momentum	2.7m
Straight rope climb (without the use of the legs)	2m
100m dash	19 seconds
500m run	1min 52 sec
1500 meter run (1.5K)	7 minutes
Lifting of a 25kg/55lb weight or stone (deadlift)	1 time
Average of both hands of 7.2kg/16lb shot put/throw	2m
100m swim	3 min 36 sec
Underwater breath hold	4 seconds

For youths under the age of 14, it is recommended to use a 4kg weight for the shot put. In that case, use the same scoring scale as for the 7.25kg/16lb weight to score 12-14 year olds' performance, using thus a 5-meter throw as the "0" baseline.

In brief, a 16-18 year old subject will have a minimal aptitude requirement of -12, a 14-16 year old of -24, and a 12-14 year old a score of -36.

The minimum required functional exercises need to be performed at any age, starting at 10 at the very least. A child ought to be able to do the exercises without any added difficulty compared to an adult, and they are equally beneficial for either child or adult to perform the rescue of a peer, to escape of self-defend against any danger. These exercises are listed as the following:

1) Recovery: to transition from a hanging extension to a hand-supported stance without the use of legs, on a beam or bar *(muscle-up variation)*.

   Weak or young individuals can regress to a recovery on their forearms, easier to execute.

2) Crossing upright, any obstacle where vertigo/fear of heights can occur: a wall or fence at least 4 meters (13 feet) off the ground.

3) Jumping off an elevation of 4 meters (13 feet) and landing any which way possible, safely. Weaker individuals or children must first hang from their hands, which considerably diminishes the height of the jump.

4) Knowledge of the various ways to assist the sick and wounded and to single-handedly transport/carry a peer of equal weight.

5) Throwing an object with dexterity. Method of testing with the following exercise: to reach with both arms, successively, a target measuring 1 square meter (a little over 3 square feet) at a distance of 20 meters (65 feet) with an object of acceptable weight, of the shape or volume of a rock, ball, stone etc…

6) Knowledge of basic strikes and punches from boxing or wrestling in order to perform attacks. The ability to neutralize and control a dangerous individual.

All the aforementioned drills, which represent the minimal requirement for someone to be considered as "coping", allow to quickly and easily determine the overall physical ability of any individual. The test subjects can either perform or not the various drills, demonstrate or not the various ways to climb or scale, swim or self-defend, skills that may have to be used at any moment.

It becomes therefore easy to determine the person's weak points and immediately direct the subject to learn the particular skills that will help them reach the desired fitness level.

An adult who, inside of one day, is incapable of entirely satisfying all conditions in order to be deemed "coping", needs to be ranked as a *physical zero*.

To get a clearer idea of the general physical condition of an individual already at "coping" level or to establish a comparison with any other individual, proceed as follows:

1) Write down exactly the person's score in each of the 12 tests on the type-card/score card. Deduce the physical aptitude score by using the scale used to analyze performance.

2) Note the extent of the person's sports knowledge and special abilities by having them perform first the most functional exercises, also considered necessary, to be ranked as "coping", which are:

   a. Weapons wielding: sword, saber, rifle or handgun.

   b. Rowing and boarding maneuvers.

   c. Horseback riding and carriage driving.

   d. Driving of mechanical vehicles like bicycle, automobile, etc.

   e. Use of common tools: hammer, file, saw, shovel, pick axe, digging tools...

CHAPTER VIII : SCORING & RECORD KEEPING

SCORE CARD EXAMPLE

EVENT	SUBJECT X Age 18 Ht 160cm Wt 56kg P.R. Score	SUBJECT Y Age 18 Ht 164cm Wt 61kg P.R. Score	SUBJECT Z Age 20 Ht 170cm Wt 65kg P.R. Score	SUBJECT W Age 23 Ht 172cm Wt 70kg P.R. Score
High Jump No Momentum	0.67m −1.30	0.86m 0.60	1.08m 3.60	1.15m 5
High Jump With Momentum	0.9m −1.00	1.17m 1.70	1.35m 4.00	1.42m 5.4
Broad Jump No Momentum	1.92m −0.80	2.15m 1.50	2.45m 4.50	2.65m 6.5
Broad Jump With Momentum	2.93m −0.14	3.90m 1.80	4.80m 4.25	5.05m 5.2
100m Sprint	15sec +0.50	14.5sec 2.00	12s4/100 5.50	12sec 7.5
500m Run	1min39s +0.25	1min33s 1.75	1min25s 4.50	1min21s 6.5
1500m Run	6min32s −1.60	5m551s 0.45	5m12s 3.80	4min48s 6.4
Straight Rope Climb	3.25m −1.75	7.5m 2.50	10m 5.00	10.75m 5.75
Shot Put 7.25kg/16lb	4.93m −0.07	6.9m 1.90	7.25m 2.25	9.78m 6.5
Deadlift 40kg/88lb	28kg −2.20	35kg −1.00	40kg 2.50 5 times	40kg 7.5 15 times
Underwater Breath Hold	3sec −3.50	12sec 0.20	38sec 2.80	1min50s 7
100m Swim	3min15s −1.25	2min52s 0.66	1min59s 5.20	1min25s 7.5
TOTAL SCORE	−12.86 Physically Inept	+14.06 Inferior Aptitude	+47.90 Superior Aptitude	+76.75 Exceptional Aptitude. Complete and perfect athlete.

RANKING, BENCHMARKS, SCORING

HIGH JUMP		HIGH JUMP		BROAD JUMP	
No momentum[1]		With momentum		No momentum[2]	
Height	Points	Height	Points	Distance	Points
0.8m	0	1m	0	2m	0
0.9m	1	1.1m	1	2.1m	1
1m	2	1.2m	2	2.2m	2
1.05m	3	1.3m	3	2.3m	3
1.1m	4	1.35m	4	2.4m	4
1.15m	5	1.4m	5	2.5m	5
etc…	etc…	etc…	etc…	etc…	etc…

BROAD JUMP		SPRINT		RUN	
With momentum		100 meters		500 meters	
Distance	Points	Time	Points	Time	Points
3m	0	16 sec.	0	1min 40sec.	0
3.5m	1	15 sec.	1	1min 36sec.	1
4m	2	14.5 sec.	2	1min 32sec.	2
4.5m	3	14 sec.	3	1min 28sec.	3
4.75m	4	13.5 sec.	4	1min 24sec.	4
5m	5	13 sec.	5	1min 24sec.	5
etc…	etc…	etc…	etc…	etc…	etc…

RUN		ROPE CLIMB[3]		SHOT PUT[4]	
1500 meters				7.25kg/16lb	
Time	Points	Distance	Points	Distance	Points
6 min.	0	5m	0	5m	0
5min 40sec.	1	6m	1	6m	1
5min 30sec.	2	7m	2	7m	2
5min 20sec.	3	8m	3	8m	3
5min 10sec.	4	9m	4	8.5m	4
5min 05sec.	5	10m	5	9m	5
etc…	etc…	etc…	etc…	etc…	etc…

DEADLIFT[5]		SWIM[6]		SWIM[7]	
Two-handed (40kg/88lb)		100 meters		Underwater breath hold	
Times	Points	Time	Points	Time	Points
1	0	3min	0	10 sec.	0
2	1	2min 48sec.	1	20 sec.	1
4	2	2min 36sec.	2	30 sec.	2
6	3	2min 24sec.	3	40 sec.	3
8	4	2min 12sec.	4	50 sec.	4
10	5	2min	5	60 sec.	5
etc…	etc…	etc…	etc…	etc…	etc…

[1] Any height is considered clear when no part of the body made contact with either the rope or the bar indicating the height. At the start of the jump with no momentum, it is forbidden to position the feet so as to create a bounce or to overstep.

[2] Distance is measured from the line of jump to the closest heel, assuming the jumper didn't fall back after the landing.

[3] The start position for the climb is seated on the ground and ascending is performed without the assistance of the legs.

[4] Momentum is generated in a 2-square meters perimeter; it is forbidden to step outside the perimeter. The throwing distance is measured from the forward line of the square to the divot created by the landing of the weight. Scoring distance is calculated by averaging a left hand and a right hand throw.

[5] Testing is performed with successive lifts, or repetitions, to full lockout of the legs. Pause between repetitions is 1 second, arms locked straight and vertical, forward leaning trunk. The negative points scale refers to lifts lighter than 40kg at a rate of 1 point for every 5kg/11lb.

[6] The swimming distance must be performed without a noticeable favorable current.

[7] The body must be fully submerged. The negative scoring scale is established with a rate of 1 point for every second under the 10-second baseline.

CHAPTER IX : HYGIENIC RECOMMENDATIONS

Training apparel. Nutritional considerations for hypothermia avoidance. Cold resistance training. Air baths. Water usage. Localized fatigue, general fatigue and being out-of-breath. General rules to delay fatigue onset.

Physical training is best performed outdoors.

Outdoor training is the principal characteristic of any rational method. Complete physical education cannot take place indoors or in an enclosed gymnasium.

There are extenuating circumstances such as: pouring rain, snow, hazardous terrain, extreme cold, violent winds etc, when obviously training will occur indoors; such training needs to be considered as the exception to the rule.

In that scenario, it is crucial to ensure proper air circulation and airing of the training facility; or, and this is preferred, to train under basic shelter: hangar, carport etc.

Physical training must never take place immediately after a meal.

In the case of moderate exercise, an hour interval is sufficient for children, but for adults, it is best to wait longer.

Anytime one wants to engage in strenuous activity or produce significant effort, it is best to wait until digestion ran its cycle, around 3 to 4 hours. It is also not recommended to perform considerable work in a fasted state in the morning.

It is necessary to remove any item of clothing that is either useless or could potentially get in the way of training.

The ideal dress is the following: shirtless, a basic pair of shorts or linen pants, long or short, held up, if necessary, by a slightly elastic belt, light shoes or simply barefoot.

Based on the weather conditions, individuals' predisposition at the moment or the kind of exercises to be performed, the addition of a light cotton t-shirt or soft shirt is permitted.

When it comes to basic exercises, clothing should in no way help correct or control movement.

Shirtless training is necessary to learn the mechanics of movement; it allows assessment of the external aspect of the body, to see weak or underdeveloped body parts, to note defects or malformations.

In a group setting this type of work allows the individuals to study one another, to observe their external development or to learn *on* the body itself the role and function of the muscles.

If only basic educational exercises are implemented, it is best to train in front of a mirror large enough to be able to study and control oneself.

To avoid rapid cooling or hypothermia after training, it is important to not wear sweat soaked clothing. One must therefore be sufficiently undressed or wear specific training apparel.

The more clothing, the easier to sweat. Sweat soaked clothes are not only the main cause of colds and bronchitis, but are also uncomfortable on the body.

Anyone that has experienced this feeling will naturally seek to avoid it in the future, after having worn too much, or forced to be dressed, when exerting lesser effort during a session. Light clothing avoids this discomfort and promotes work capacity production.

Cold training/resilience is performed as such:

1) Air baths, in the daylight or sun, in all seasons, shirtless.

2) Cold baths.

3) All sorts of ablutions, local or general, as well as the following process, which is very effective: barefoot walk in cold water or in the morning dew, on a humid surface.

Cold training resistance is essential.

Group of children ages 8-11 beginning a session with walking exercises with corrective movement, wearing only shorts. Air baths (head, trunk and limbs exposed) constitute a formidable way to train resistance against poor weather, among other benefits.

(...)

Rest and fatigue management is necessary in order for the body to restart.

One must consider:

1) Localized fatigue.

2) General fatigue.

3) Being out-of-breath (*breathlessness*)

Localized fatigue results in the overtraining of a particular body part. At a certain level, it promotes muscular soreness, which manifests itself as a certain tightness in the muscles or a sharp pain during contraction.

Experience shows that simple soreness goes away within forty-eight hours, by allowing the tired muscles to recover, more or less.

Properly executed massage may diminish the duration of soreness.

Localized soreness is not an indicator of severe impairment; it must be treated as an indicator to stop the session. It usually appears following the practice of a new exercise, which engages muscles that have been inactive for a while.

General fatigue can be felt throughout the body. It presents three main levels: *lassitude* (lack of energy), *overworking* and *forcing*.

Lassitude or light fatigue disappears generally after a hearty meal, a few hours of sleep (napping) or normal nighttime sleep. It can at times happen with a bit of fever, insomnia or lack of appetite. Even with the latter, additional rest will reset the body.

Overworking occurs when one is still experiencing fatigue/lassitude and continues training regardless. The body didn't have the necessary amount of time to reset to satisfaction and to mend itself. Symptoms a little worse than those of lassitude can occur, especially if the overworking period is prolonged. The body worsens on a daily basis and offers less resistance to disease.

Forcing, or highest level of fatigue, is the consequence of a last ditch effort of will power to perform excessive work, the body already being in an overworked state. Muscles stiffen and stop responding to commands. Timing is generally off and in some cases, consequences can be fatal.

Breathlessness is a cardiopulmonary symptom resulting from an excessive energy expenditure in a short amount of time. In this state, breathing is obstructed, the heart beats quickly; there can even be suffocation with the complete inability to breathe. The lungs are then saturated with carbon dioxide, which they are unable to expel. This occurs mainly during running. The suffocating runner experiences the early stages of asphyxia. As soon as symptoms of breathlessness occur, immediately cease activity and restore calm through breathing exercises or a slow walk, preferably walking on the toes.

Rules concerning the alternating of rest and work periods are applicable to the entire day, not just the time specifically dedicated to physical training. Rest periods need to be regulated in such a way that at the start of every training session, any traces of fatigue need to have dissipated.

Warning signs that one may have gone beyond the limits:

Fever, insomnia or restless sleep, irritability, lack of appetite, digestive troubles, tiredness upon waking, excessive soreness, weakness in the legs etc.

Specific indicators to stop training are:

General stiffness, limbs shaking, loss of color/pale face or extreme redness, repeated breathlessness.

After a full day, the level of fatigue should only be light, which a good night's sleep ought to fully eradicate.

Positive signs that indicate a well regulated dose of training are:

Hearty appetite, deep sleep, sensation of well-being upon waking and the absence of soreness.

Every individual possess a different threshold of resistance. One needs to learn how to recognize and know one's strength in order to not exceed it or waste it.

The limits of fatigue, as well as breathlessness, can be considerably pushed back with training, adaptation to work capacity, the regularity of respiratory movements, a balanced diet, well-spread doses of rest and recovery, a proper rhythm in work performance.

Resistance differs for a single individual based on their disposition at that given moment in time. Fasting, all-nighters, outside temperature and/or emotions are the main causes, which make one's resilience and performance vary greatly.

CHAPTER X : CONDUCTING GROUP INSTRUCTION

Group repetition. Study lessons and Real Life lessons. General rules regarding individual training. General rules regarding group training.

In order to train a large group of subjects at once, begin by spreading them in groups as small as possible (8 to 10 students max). Students within a group need to be of approximately equal strength. Each group is placed under the direction of an instructor or someone sufficiently capable.

For the teaching of basic educational exercises, the students are placed in each group next to one another, in one or two rows, at intervals and distances such that they can move freely. The quincunx formation offers the advantage of requiring less space, and promotes keeping a watchful eye.

Students often need to be placed face-to-face to increase their interest and allow them to assess each other.

In the teaching of other drills, students are positioned in the most convenient and practical way.

Additionally, explanations and observations need to be reduced to the necessary minimum *(Translator's note: minimal cueing by using simplest commands possible)*.

The general hygienic benefits depend mostly on the care brought to the regulation of physical energy expenditure, meaning the way the instructor conducts the lesson.

So, for instance, for a lesson of a total duration of 25 minutes, each student is required to deliver 20 to 22 minutes of actual work.

Rest periods must be frequent, but extremely brief (10 to 20 seconds on average).

During the educational lessons, instruction is mainly individual.

The teacher/master successively tests each student and corrects their posture, front and especially profile.

The biggest errors are corrected first; then, minor errors. For instance, in the following move of *straight leg forward elevation,* attention needs to be directed first by the instructor to the *body's position* and <u>not</u> the height of the leg. The master should only allow a short amount of time per move, and try it again later, in order to not wear out the attention span of the students.

Whenever the master needs to ensure a correct active posture, he orders: "this move, maintain posture". Students adopt the posture and maintain it until further instruction.

During the *Real Life lessons*, instruction is conducted collectively, meaning with the entire class, either broken up by groups or by reuniting all the groups under the orders of the master at any given time during the lesson.

Group training begins as soon as the movements are performed individually with the utmost attention to correct form. It then just about becomes the exclusive way to train. Going back to individual training occurs only if it appears necessary to correct the execution of certain movements.

Group training is useful for:
1) Assessing at a glance the way movements are understood and performed.
2) Getting a precise idea of the speed of movement and thus establish a uniform cadence.

3) Stimulating the students and promote more intense effort from the less energetic ones.

4) Avoiding any waste of time.

The master instructor needs to pay attention so that the group training of the basic educational exercises doesn't regress to general "sketches" of the ordered movement. To achieve that, he prolongs stopping time by frequently commanding: "maintain posture" or simply "halt!" in order to verify correct dynamic form.

During the execution of the basic educational exercises, students never count out loud; *they focus their attention on proper breathing.*

Only the master instructor commands the cadence out loud, himself thus regulating the duration of each pause and deciding on the "count".

Group session. Execution of backwards slit move with hands on hips.

The execution of each movement takes place in two ways:

1) *Upon command*: the master announces the movement without having to demonstrate it, then commands the action: "this move, at my command". The students then begin at the cadence given to them, or without cadence at the command "Go!"

2) *By emulation/imitation*: the master announces the movement, then commands "this movement, imitate". The students look the master in the eye and imitate his movements precisely and accurately.

The latter fashion is mostly used in the beginning; it prevents waste of time by eliminating many an explanation. It is mainly used for the execution of preliminary exercises as well as breathing exercises.

Movements end at the command "Halt!" or "Cease". When a drill has a starting position other than the Upright Posture, the master indicates the starting position.

At the "Halt!" or "Cease!" command, students always return to the starting position.

All group instruction needs to be based on emulation/imitation.

The master encourages good will *(Translator's note: a sense of pride and ownership in participation and execution)*, relays to everyone the importance of the hygienic and functional benefits of the exercises and promotes *personal best effort* as much as possible, particularly during runs or marches. He stimulates periodically self-confidence by setting up mini contests or competitions. The classic tests listed in Chapter VII serve these contests best; the master can also created events based on circumstances.

Group training of functional exercises: rope assisted wall scaling.

Generally, the hours dedicated to physical education are limited. The master's main preoccupation lies in using those hours efficiently and have them produce maximal effect. In order to do so, the master instructor must constantly require:

1) That students adopt good posture habitually and constantly, as well as positive attitude.

2) That each short distance coverage (maximum 100 meters) be done as a brisk march or run, without concern for alignment, so that each student can freely go at their own speed. This prescription constitutes one element of *energy education*; it challenges speed weakness in heavier set individuals and makes them adopt a slower pace in line with their physique.

A heavy pace or movement comes from the central nervous system, which acts as if "asleep", which needs to be "awakened" by exercises of *rapid relaxation* (*Translator's note: also know as fast and loose drills*).

3) That in each displacement (to get to a determined location), a few minutes of jogging at an appropriate pace need to be done according to outside temperature, load carrying and apparel worn (*load resistance education by racing*).

4) That parameters relative to marching or running be rigorously observed at all times *(walking and running education)*. Displacement are generally numerous enough inside of one session or day, so as to not having to dedicate a specialized session for them.

5) That the duration of each rest between exercises be reduced to the bare minimum.

6) That for any exercises done using equipment, the maximal amount of students need to be trained at once. The master instructor cues the others with another exercise, if numbers are too large, while they wait their turn.

The master instructor registers every performance of every one of his students on the *scorecard,* later used for results analysis and physical aptitude measurement, where the cumulative scores of the 12 tests are recorded (see Chapter VII). The scores and performances are recorded as accurately as possible at specific dates, about once a quarter. Individual score cards need to also contain a chart summarizing the overall results achieved after each new performance test. This chart can be based on the following model:

DATE	NUMBER Total students	APTITUDE Insufficient	APTITUDE Sufficient	APTITUDE Average	APTITUDE Superior	APTITUDE Exceptional	TOTAL Scores of all students	AVERAGE	FINDINGS
OCTOBER 1	50	28	19	3	0	0	130	+2.6	
FEBRUARY 1	50	12	28	8	2	0	280	+5.6	
JUNE 1	50	6	27	12	4	1	612	+12.24	
SEPTEMBER 30	50	1	12	23	9	5	775.5	+15.5	

The calculation of the total points is done by simply adding up the scores of all the students. The mean, or average, is deduced from the total and hence provides a precise idea of the general physical ability of the students as a group.

CHAPTER XI : FIELD ORGANIZATION FOR THE PRACTICE OF PHYSICAL EXERCISES

General layout of the field for physical exercises. Necessary equipment. Assigned special locations. Economical organization. Use of any non-prepared field.

In order to physically educate a large number of students at once, it is absolutely necessary to have access to an appropriate field that has been judiciously organized and laid out (fig. 17, 18 and 19).

No specific field shape is recommended in particular. However, when given a choice, the simplest shape, i.e. a square or rectangle, is most practical.

When it comes to the surface, the best one is usually a beaten dirt ground covered with a thin layer of sand or fine gravel. Sand, particularly sea sand, ensures quick drying after rain.

Dimensions given to a field don't have to be precise; they depend on the number of students exercising at once.

In general, school or military courtyards, playgrounds, fields for maneuvers, aswell as certain public spaces, are perfectly adequate and can be easily turned into physical training areas.

As a rule, a *complete* field, meaning one that's set up to promote the teaching and practice of all exercises, contains:

1) A circular track for distance runs.
2) A straight track for sprints.

3) Various jumping stations in sufficient numbers for high jumps, long jumps and broad jumps.

4) A free space for games and group training.

5) Suspension/off ground training equipment, as well as scaling/climbing equipment, which are, in order of importance: any type of bar, angled straight climbing ropes, climbing platforms, ladders, walls etc.

6) Beams or horizontal bars of varying height for balancing drills, hand supported jumps, some scaling drills and hazardous obstacle clearance.

7) A track with various obstacles to clear (fig 22)

8) Objects such as: stones, bars, weights, dumbbells, weighted bags etc., for lifting exercises.

9) An assigned spot for objects ranging from 4kg to 20kg (9lb to 44lb) such as: stones, weights, shot put for throwing exercises

10) A target with light objects such as rocks, balls, stones, pebbles for target practice.

11) A wrestling or boxing area.

12) An area with elevation to overcome vertigo or fear of heights.

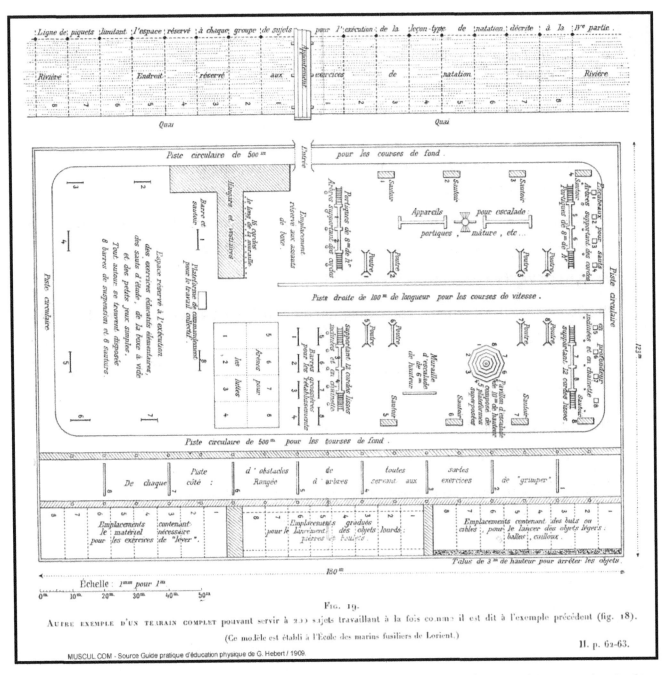

Schematic of a small area (15m X 20m, like a school courtyard) turned into a physical training field. This field can easily accommodate two groups of 10-15 people, thus 20-30 people training at once. While one group uses the center open free space, the other group can move from station to station. Whenever space is restricted, it is necessary to utilize the available resources to the fullest, such as using nearby structures for suspension work, ropes or any other climbing equipment. It is up to the organizer to show ingenuity by arranging the field as practically and economically to satisfy the needs of a complete training session. The pool (upper right rectangle) is only here to indicate a good placement for it. It is exceptional and rare to have a proximal area to practice swimming drills.

The aforementioned organization is relatively easy to set up and requires little cost.

Indeed:

- #1 & #2 need only a basic outlined track, which can be delineated with pickets.
- A high jump station for #3 needs only 2 pickets with markings one centimeter apart and a rope to indicate height.

For long or broad jumps, a layer of sand consists of dimensions about 6-meters long, 2-meters wide and 20-centimeters thick. Distance cleared can be measured by horizontal markings on the border.

For depth jumps or higher jumps, use ladders, stools, scales, mounds etc.

The free space area for #4 only needs to be outlined.

For #5, suspension/off-ground gear such as bars, ropes etc. can be economically installed by anchoring on trees, walls or any kind of post. Additionally, these anchor points can also be used for climbing.

Beams or horizontal bars are made of various pieces of wood, preferably cylindrical, placed on A-frames or rested on mounds at least 1-meter high.

The track for the obstacle course is comprised of ditches, wooden fences, and dirt or stone mounds. It is mainly a question of terrain.

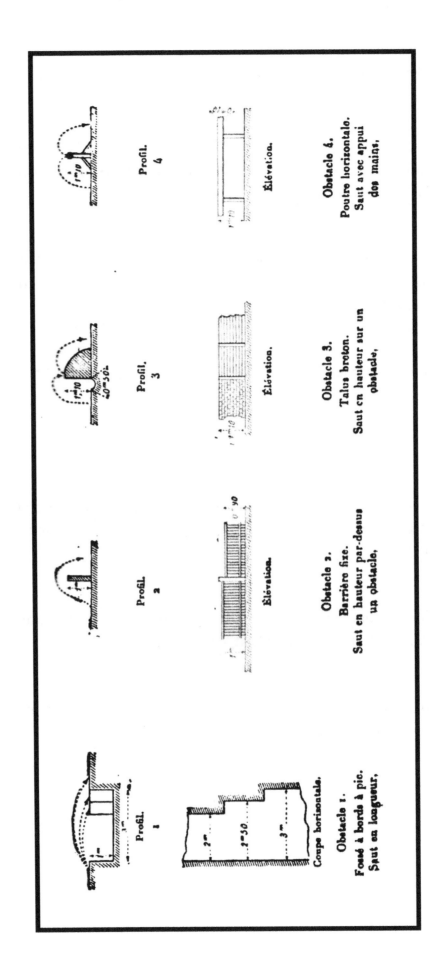

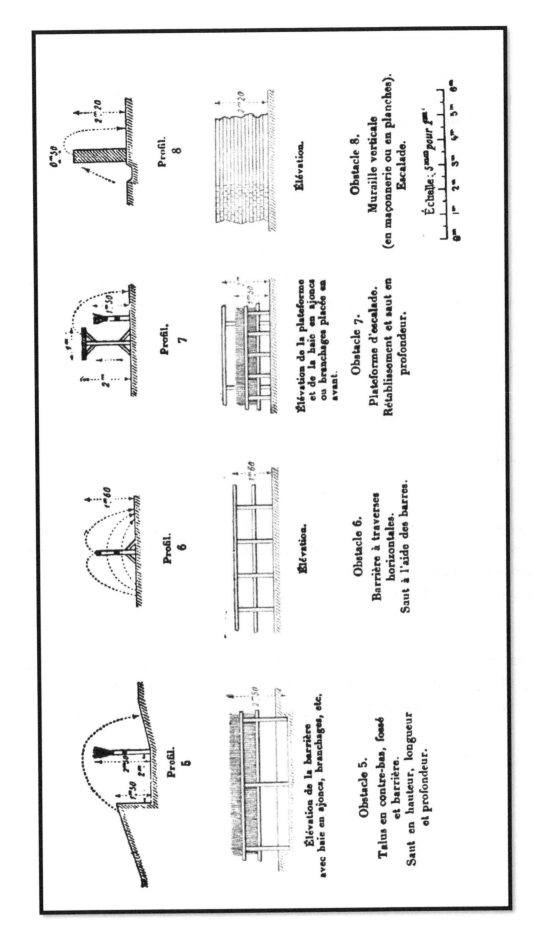

For lifting exercises, one can use any heavy objects such as: big rocks, iron or cast iron weights, bars, bags filled with sawdust or sand, etc., to avoid the expense of barbells, dumbbells or other weights.

When it comes to throwing weights, the only need is to get a hold of an object of any shape or size (weighing from 4 to 20 kg) and to have a few balls weighted at 7.25kg (16lb.)

For projectile throwing for target practice, all that is needed is to make a wooden target measuring 1 square meter approximately or to draw a target on a wall, for instance.

Wrestling arenas are set up by spreading a layer of sod or sawdust on the ground.

Finally, for overcoming fear of heights, any sort of construction, apparatus or various trees can be used.

The amount of spots or equipment placed on the training field depends on the available resources, as well as the number of individuals to train at once. In general, in a perfectly organized field or setting, dispositions are such that each working group possesses access to a complete gym of its own.

Such a placement allows the different groups, under the commands of one instructor, to not only all train at the same time, but also to perform the same exercises in the same instance, which greatly facilitates the observation and leading of the session.

Considering for instance a total of 50 people, divided into groups of 10, each group would have access to:

- A jumping station.
- One or several climbing walls.
- A horizontal beam.
- Weights, bars or stones for lifting.
- A specified spot for throwing, with stones, rocks, weights etc.
- A wrestling area.
- Running tracks and obstacle courses can always be used for all the groups.

When the dimensions of the accessible field or the available resources are insufficient, the set-ups requiring priority over all others are, in order of importance:

1) Jumping stations.
2) Running track.
3) Hanging/Suspension or climbing apparatuses.

All of this to at least be able to: run, climb and jump during a session. Then, in order of importance, come objects for lifting and throwing, the wrestling area etc.

Use of a tree for all scaling and climbing exercises, as well as elevation training.

A master instructor ought to be able to draw from the first available field and be resourceful to train his students. With a little ingenuity, any kind of field or terrain not specifically prepared, such as school playground, courtyard, meadow, clearing etc., can be instantly turned into a physical training area. In that spirit:

1) Use open spaces for the basic educational exercises. Boxing, wrestling, jumping, sprinting and all games.

2) Use trees, walls, columns, ladders etc. for climbing, or scaling.

3) Choose appropriately sized rocks for lifting and throwing.

4) Use ditches, mounds etc. for obstacle courses.

For a fully "naked" field, the following exercises need always be performed:

1) Basic educational exercises (minus off ground training/suspension).
2) High jumps and long jumps.
3) Sprints and distance runs.
4) Shadow boxing, sparring and combative techniques.
5) The study of strikes and counters, as well as wrestling if there is grass or sand.
6) Rescue and carrying of wounded individuals training.
7) Lifting and throwing, since rocks can always be found for either.
8) Games.

SPECIAL THANKS

I want to thank Dr Ed Thomas for the impetus to translate and transcribe Georges Hébert's work. The influence of Dr Thomas in the fitness community about digging in the past for some of the most compelling forms of training that withstood time and have been diluted over time, if not extinct in some cases, doesn't only affect my philosophy of training, but that of many peers who happened to have steered me towards Dr Thomas' path. I've had the pleasure to help him teach an Indian Clubs certification and led one of the teams of candidates. Ed was generous in letting some of the team leaders and other friends hold specialized workshops where we were able to "showcase our own goods". For me, it was a demonstration of a product of my invention, the SmartFlex™, for which Indian Clubs training brought the device its missing link before I decided to proceed with the prototype and its ensuing venture.

I decided not to deviate from the words, despite any advances in technology, research or even opinions of current well-educated experts, because this work is both a work of History and fundamentals, essential principles of fitness, which are timeless, true and proven. Hébert himself acknowledges that in the Preface of the book.

Furthermore, I want to thank my friend in fitness James Neidlinger who first introduced me to Indian clubs, which led to me taking an Indian clubs certification workshop with Brett Jones, another influencer in my career. Brett taught me to simplify and systemize training, with progressions and regressions that are user friendly yet dramatically enhancing performance *naturally* in the system I created for my invention, the FAST system for SmartFlex™ (Flexibility Agility Strength Tonus), which will be the subject of a companion book to the second part of Hébert's trilogy.

In the *Noble Purpose* crew, Ron Jones and his co-horts the Lean Berets also have been instrumental in their own deep research of American fitness Historical influencers such as Stan LeProtti and LaSierra High School's training standards, which he is bringing out through an upcoming documentary. I was amazed to see the similarities and congruence in those older training methods which have waned over generations.

Fitness Peers like Paul Daniels and Ruben Cervantes, who have been willing subjects to experiment on, physically validated the theories from this book for me before applying them on their own clients

My clients, of course, have been key to the field work associated with *The Natural Method*, as they have validated my research simply with their feedback, joyful movements, improved performance and athleticism at a markedly quick rate since the introduction of Hébert's method (sometimes aided by the SmartFlex™ which helps *deliver the information* to the body more quickly).

I want to thank Yannick d'Assignies for his skill in marketing, formatting and putting together the publication of this book, something I would have never been able to accomplish from a technical standpoint.

Finally, I want to thank my wife Noëlle and my two sons, Fletcher and Branson, to whom I dedicate this series. Their patience and support in allowing me to pursue this series of books transcends any financial prospects, as this is a calling than a get-rich process. This work is so important it needed to be translated so that future generations can have access to it.

Made in the USA
Middletown, DE
29 September 2024